Pr

Surviving Widowhood

Surviving Widowhood is a heartfelt book of hope for anyone walking through the grief of losing a spouse. Sharing openly about their struggles, Sharon and Lori throw back the curtains of their own lives and heartache to show how God met them in their pain and provided comfort through it all. These touching devotionals will serve as a balm for the hurting heart no matter where a widow is in her grieving journey.

> —Lori Wilhite, founder of Leading and Loving It,
> author of *Ephesians: Head Held High*

Surviving Widowhood is an incredible book which offers genuine hope to widows. I appreciate how transparent, honest, and open Sharon and Lori are as they share their hearts and raw emotions in this journey called "widowhood." The devotions are short, powerful, encouraging, and relatable. Each devotion ends with helpful, practical applications: prayer, perspective, and prompts. Sharon and Lori remind us that our hope is in God. "Through it all, we learn to trust in Jesus, we learn to trust in God, and we learn to depend upon His Word." *Surviving Widowhood* will be a blessing and encouragement to every widow, regardless of where they are in their journey or season in life. I've been a widow for thirteen years, and it deeply ministered to my heart. I plan to give it to every widow I know and keep many copies on hand to give to those I have not yet met.

> —Sara Beekman, speaker, president of
> *Stop to Pray Ministries*, and friend

From the moment I received that heart-wrenching knock at my front door and found out that my military husband had been killed in combat, I knew more than ever that the only way I would survive was to cling to my faith in Christ. Though many people came alongside to help me through the dark days of grief and the single parenting of our five young children, I ultimately knew it would only be the Lord who truly could repair our broken hearts—and only other widows that could possibly understand the depth of my sorrow. The words Sharon and Lori penned in this book are inspired, honest, and written from their own seasons of pain. Each chapter brings comfort and hope to widows of all ages and stages of life.

—Ginger Ravella, author of *Hope Found*,
co-founder of Never Alone Widows Retreats

Sharon and Lori are trusted voices for women who find themselves on a road unplanned, unwelcomed, and unwanted: widowhood. Their godly and practical wisdom in *Surviving Widowhood* is like a daily latte of hope and help.

—Pam Farrel, author of fifty-five books, including, the bestselling
Men Are Like Waffles, Women Are Like Spaghetti

Most women don't plan for widowhood. The loss of a spouse changes everything and is hard to get through. Because loss is a hard road and the grief process tricky to navigate, it takes someone who has walked that path to reach out the hand of hope. Authors Sharon Engram and Lori Rohlinger reach their readers with understanding and tenderness, offering help to those walking the journey that no one wants to talk about but so many are trying to navigate. The perfect book for those grieving or to gift to someone who is.

—Debbie Alsdorf, author of *Deeper, A Woman Who Trusts God* and *It's Momplicated*

Loneliness finds a companion, grief finds a friend, heartache finds a promise, and a soul finds healing on the pages of this devotional. Sharon and Lori speak real words with raw emotions as their journey through widowhood uncovers the soul. Whether you are experiencing loss or gifting this book to a dear friend, the words contained on these pages will bring a soothing balm of relief to her weary heart. Encouragement from two women who fully grasp the deep anguish overwhelming every ounce of your being. Within these pages hope is exposed and experienced even on the darkest of days. When no one else understands . . . when you are feeling all alone . . . allow these precious friends to speak into those hidden parts and remind you there is indeed a reason to take your next breath in *Surviving Widowhood*.

—Carol Tetzlaff, author of *Ezra: Unleashing the Power of Praise*

This book is perfect for anyone who has lost the love of her life, her champion, her friend, her husband. Sharon Engram and Lori Rohlinger have created a powerful, yet bite-sized, devotional that is a perfect gift when there are no words to ease someone's grief. Insightful and encouraging words fill the pages of this book in a way that every widow can use and appreciate. This devotional will help widows survive the lonely walk of grief by drawing closer to God in a manageable way, not overwhelming or asking too much of the grieving wife. It's a delicate balance to minister to the grieving, but this book has done it beautifully!

—Kim Erickson, grieving mom and author of *Surviving Sorrow:
A Mother's Guide to Living with Loss* and *His Last Words:
What Jesus Taught and Prayed in His Final Hours (John 13-17)*

In *Surviving Widowhood*, Sharon and Lori candidly share their personal journeys through the painful loss of their husbands, and the hope and healing they each have found in the timeless promises tucked away in God's Word. Listen closely, and you will hear one recurring theme woven into both of their stories: the calm assurance that one day they will be together again ... for eternity!

—David and Sharon Culross, lifelong friends
and ministry partners

Like a tender squeeze of your hand, reminding you that you are not alone, these beautiful devotions provide the gift of hope to a grieving heart.

—Erica Wiggenhorn, author of *Letting God Be Enough*

Surviving Widowhood strikes a tender balance between the pain of loss and the comfort of Jesus-breathed hope. Not only do its pages offer the reader a safe place to fall, but they also give her a gift incalculable—the grace of knowing she is never alone.

—Sara Cormany, author, speaker, and friend

Everyone has unique life experiences. Some are joyful and others are painfully scarring. What we do with these experiences changes the direction by which we live and affects the direction of those around us. Having watched closely as Lori has faced her life experiences, which have been horrific to say the least, I have seen firsthand how her joy has been steady through grief and sadness. She has walked with grace and purpose in order to guide others in similar experiences. God has used her life as a beacon of hope for those who are overwhelmed with grief and sadness. Having an example to follow, having a plan to put into action, is a gift when facing the unknown journey of widowhood. Lori and Sharon share their experiences of love, loss, and hope so beautifully and inspirationally so that others may be strengthened and encouraged as they face life as a widow.

—Lisa Young, author of the *New York Times* best seller,
Sexperiment: 7 Days to Lasting Intimacy with Your Spouse

surviving widowhood

surviving
widowhood

40 DEVOTIONS
of Hope

Sharon Engram & Lori Rohlinger

Redemption Press. PO Box 427, Enumclaw, WA 98022
Toll-Free (844) 2REDEEM (273-3336)

ISBN 13: 978-1-64645-668-0 (Paperback)
        978-1-64645-670-3 (Hardcover)
        978-1-64645-671-0 (ePub)
        978-1-64645-669-7 (Mobi)

LCCN: 2021924721

Lori's Dedication

To Jacob, Zachary, Joshua, and Brooke (a.k.a. the Linger Dingers). Dad and I love you so much, and you inspire me to be a better mom each day. Thank you for helping me take care of your dad and loving me in my grief. Love you (and you too, Greg). Always and forever.

Sharon's Dedication

In loving memory of my husband, Don, the love of my life for sixty years. You led our family with fun, adventure, wisdom, and love. You faithfully served God, sharing Jesus across the world. Thanks for being my biggest cheerleader, and I'm so glad I got to do life with you. Miss you every day.

Contents

Acknowledgments

We are deeply grateful to Kim Erickson—thank you for all your hard work in helping to get this book organized. We couldn't have done it without you and your encouragement.

We are grateful for our family member Lydia Engram, who edited devotionals until she was cross-eyed. We love you!

We are most grateful for Jesus, who has given us hope in our widow's journey. We'd like to thank everyone at Redemption Press for their incredible help to us on this book. Thanks to Athena, Dori, Sara, Micah, Tisha, and Staci—you all are rock stars!

I'm so thankful for my children who have not only been here to support me in my grief journey but have also grieved the loss of their dad: Ric, Steve, Shari, and Lori, and to my daughters-in-love, Sally and Tami. To my grandchildren (Lindsay, Jacqui, James, Mitchell, JJ, Kylee,

Micah, Jacob, Alli, Tori, Zachary, Trenton, Joshua, and Brooke) and great-grandchildren (Peter, Teddy, Leanor, Benji, Josie, Mae, and Willow)—I love you so much.

Sharon Rae, your friendship helped carry me through the hard early months as you came to visit, you encouraged me, and listened to my many tearful phone calls.

Thank you, Cheri and Kim, for creating Driveway Divas during COVID so we could be together during my early months of aloneness.

A huge thank you to Erica, Carol, Pam, Debbie, Ginger, and the She Writes for Him tribe for your encouragement to keep writing this devotional for widows. Also, my Velcro Sisters and Lois Legacy 2 ladies.

~Sharon

Thanks to Mel, Mick, and Stephie. I couldn't do life without you.

Thanks to my sister, Shari, for the hours of listening and excellent question asking to help me spread my wings and move forward.

Thanks to Dr. Jen Bellingrodt for the wise counsel, coffee dates, crying sessions, and being my friend. And thanks for thinking that God really trusts me.

~Lori

A Note to You, Precious Widow

 $\mathcal{W}$ e understand your broken heart and want to share encouragement with you. I'm glad you are holding these devotionals in your hands, and I am praying they will bring comfort to you in your time of sorrow.

There is no way to prepare for becoming a widow. You may have lost your husband suddenly, or like me, you had a few months to say goodbye. When my husband, Don, was first diagnosed with cancer, we were told he had two weeks to two months to live. God graciously gave us two years.

Yet on the day he died, I was not ready, nor was I prepared.

I had never heard of "widows' fog," but it quickly overtook me. I found it hard to think and make decisions. Ever so slowly, the "fog" of widowhood began to lift, and I wished for a small devotional book written by a widow for a widow. I wanted something that would be short, not lengthy, from the heart of another widow. I wanted someone who was ahead of me on her grief journey to give my broken heart hope and encouragement.

I sensed the Lord nudging me to journal and write. Out of this nudging have come these devotionals. These devotionals are personal, sharing from my heart the grief and adjustments I have experienced as a new widow. Each devotion is wrapped in Scripture to bring hope and encouragement as you lean into the arms of Jesus, who is the Healer of broken hearts.

"Weeping may endure for a night, but joy comes in the morning" (Psalm 30:5 NKJV).

Each of the forty devotionals is followed with a page to journal your thoughts and feelings. It may be only a word or a sentence, but I encourage you to date it so when you reread it later, you'll gradually realize you *are* moving forward.

Give yourself grace. Grief is very personal, and there is no time schedule for its end. I'm praying for you.

Love,

Sharon

Dear Widow

*A*s you read this book, please know that we had you in mind. While we don't know each other personally, I can touch the pain you are going through. Each of us are uniquely created by our Creator, and while we may experience the same grief, it doesn't mean we will process it the same way. And that's okay.

Please never judge yourself by how someone else has gone through loss. Understand that God works in very different ways for very distinct purposes. He has a plan and a purpose uniquely for your life.

And if you are a widow with children still in the home, I know how challenging, lonely, isolating, and overwhelming this journey will be. When my husband was first diagnosed, my children ranged from ages five to thirteen, so I know what it is like to have a young one on your lap and also deal with those hard teenage years. Because of Greg's quickly diminishing health, I faced single parenting before the grief of widowhood was a reality. But there is hope! We have a personal God who knows what's happening in your life right now, and He cares about you and your children. Focus on today, and not yesterday or tomorrow, and He will see you through.

While the journal page can seem overwhelming, we put it in there because it's so important in your days ahead to be able to see the process you've walked through. You can even write a date on the page if that's all you can do. When you come back to it again, you will see the progress you've made.

When my mom came to me with this book idea, I had already spent a few years blogging and podcasting my pain. I was excited to write something in a "bite size" format because in those early days of grief, it was hard for me to read anything that took me more than a few minutes. My prayer is that when you read the real and raw feelings and issues that I faced—and then the Scripture that God used to speak to me—that He would use them to speak to you, too, giving you hope that only He can provide and filling you with a peace that passes all understanding.

You are loved,

Lori

Foreword

$\mathcal{G}$rief, loss, sadness, loneliness, despair, disorientation, confusion, hopelessness came out of nowhere, and I felt it all. I was twenty-eight years old and in a great season of life. My wife and I had been married for four years, and she was eight months pregnant with our first child. The pregnancy had gone better than expected with little morning sickness or discomfort. We were so excited about the birth of our firstborn, and we were moving toward a transition in our ministry career that promised growth and development.

The story began in late March 1988 when we drove my parents, Don and Sharon, along with my then teenage sister, Lori, to the airport because they were moving across country to Phoenix, Arizona, for a new job. As the plane pushed back from the gate, I turned to look at my wife, and she seemed pale and weak. We ended up taking her to the doctor's office, where they discovered she had preeclampsia but assured us they had it under control.

During the night, my son decided to come into this world, but in the process of his birth, complications happened to my wife. She ended up suffering a major stroke, and two days later, she was at home with her Lord. I was left with a three-day old baby to raise by myself. My life had crumbled before my eyes. My mother and sister moved back to Northern Ohio to take care of my baby and stand with me as I grieved the loss of my wife.

The authors of this book on widowhood are those two ladies who were of indispensable help and strength to me during my time of loss. Sadly, they now have had to walk through the grief process themselves as both have become widows in the past few years—my mom after sixty years of marriage with my father, and my sister after almost twenty-two years of marriage (to her husband who died of rare neurological disease), and she was then left to single parent four children.

Right now, you may be thinking that's a lot of loss, and you don't need more sadness in your life. I get it, but this book is not a book focused on death and loss. It is a book that is focused on hope and comfort, strength, and peace. It is a book that points you to the One who will walk with you through your loss, who will give you the grace to grieve, and the hope to heal if you will lean into Him.

Forty short devotional thoughts for those moments when you think the pain is too overwhelming. Encouragement for when those rogue waves of grief seemingly come out of nowhere and knock you down when you think you are making progress.

I am so sorry for you in your loss, as it is a terrible road to travel. But there is hope of a better day! Being thirty-three years down the road from losing my wife, I am a testimony to the grace and faithfulness of God. He has been faithful to me. He has been faithful to my mom and sister. He will be faithful to you! Lean into Him and allow these Scriptures and stories to lead you into His comfort.

Steve Engram
Senior Pastor
Desert Springs Community Church
Goodyear, Arizona

1

Hope
(Lori)

*May the God of hope fill you with all joy and
peace in believing, so that by the power of the
Holy Spirit you may abound in hope.*
Romans 15:13

I think the one thing every widow wants in the midst
of grief is the promise that hope is on the horizon.
There has been so much loss, so much grief, and so much
pain that the thought of hope feels like a fresh breeze
blowing in your face when you can't catch your breath.
Hope is what makes tomorrow feel possible.

Romans 15:13 offers a prayer for God's people to
have hope. This is not just getting by in hope or believing that it might be on the way. No! God wants you to
abound in it. The definition of "abound" means to have
a great quantity or to have plenty. This is such a strange

concept for me as a widow because in loss and grief, there seems to be plenty of misery but not a lot of hope. God wants to make a difference in our grieving. He wants us to have an abundance of hope.

If you are a Christian, the Holy Spirit lives inside of you. He guides and directs you every day. He wants to fill you with joy and peace and hope! Don't those sound like wonderful things to be filled with instead of the pain?

So how do we tap into the hope that is available to us? By getting to know the source of hope, Jesus. Reading the Bible is where we find out more about Him, but sometimes that can feel overwhelming. You can start small by reading a couple of verses a day. Psalms is a great place to start. There is an awesome app you can download on your phone called YouVersion. You can have the Word of God at your fingertips, and they have amazing Bible studies that will give you hope in your grief.

Another great way to get to know Jesus more is through prayer. Even a simple prayer telling Him you need help will open the door of communication with Him.

Dear widow, don't give up! Hope is there for you to tap into, to lead you and guide you.

Prayer: *Lord*, give us strength for today and hope for tomorrow. Help us to let You in and push ourselves to know You more through Your Word each day. Fill us with Your joy and peace and help us to abound in Your hope!

Perspective: Hope can feel like such an elusive feeling when you are a widow, but the Bible tells us that God wants to fill us up with an abundance of hope.

Prompt: Having hope is something that personally came hard for me. How could I possibly have hope for the future when all I wanted was the past? For me, I know I needed hope to be a better mom to my kids—to realize my own strengths that weren't tied to my husband. As you sit and think about a life without your spouse, what areas would you like to see hope abound in? Ask God to give you a picture of what having hope would look like in your life a month from now, six months from now, a year from now and write those things down.

2

Tears

(Sharon)

You keep track of all my sorrows.
You have collected all my tears in your bottle.
You have recorded each one.
Psalm 56:8 NLT

*T*ears, flowing so freely. Many times, when I wasn't expecting them, the tears came. They were my constant companion after the death of my husband, Don.

A few months prior, we had celebrated our sixtieth wedding anniversary with a wonderful reception given by our children. It was a beautiful, sunny day, and many of our friends and family came to celebrate. God had graciously blessed us with extra time after Don received the diagnosis of cancer, and we were thankful to celebrate this milestone anniversary.

Now I live with memories and tears of the life we shared together. But I'm so grateful to God for this marvelous way He has equipped me for expressing my emotions. The tears I have shed have been so cleansing in my life, and after talking with other widows, I know it helps them too. I have read how emotional tears heal the heart. Tears are God's gift to us in Psalm 56:8. Oh, how much God loves me to have provided tears for me to shed!

A friend sent me a sweet gift shortly after Don's death that contained a four-inch bottle with a tag that read, "Bottle of Tears" (and you'll never guess which Scripture verse was on the bottle: Psalm 56:8). I keep it on my office desk as a constant reminder of God's compassionate love for me.

Another Scripture verse I love is a wonderful promise that "He will wipe away every tear from [our] eyes" (Revelation 21:4). I'm looking forward to that day when my tears will be wiped away, and I will experience joy without sorrow in the presence of Jesus.

Tears

Prayer: *Thank You, Heavenly Father,* that the tears I cry are precious to You, and You hold each one in a heavenly bottle.

Perspective: Tears are a natural part of grief. Each tear we shed is precious to God.

Prompt: Journal about how your tears affect you. Some people find them cleansing, while others hate to cry and may resent them. Think about the fact that God keeps your tears because they are so precious to Him. How does that make you feel toward Him?

3

Shipwrecked

(Lori)

My grace is all you need.
My power works best in weakness.
2 Corinthians 12:9 NLT

For me, being a widow has felt like being a lone survivor of a shipwreck. There was pain, panic, stress, and trauma, and then there was nothing—floating all alone in the middle of a great ocean of numbness and indecision with no land in sight. I had a life jacket, which was Jesus, but even so, the waves washed over me and threatened to drown me. I would cry out to God in desperate need, in fear, or even in anger sometimes. I couldn't believe God had let me go through this tragedy, losing the love of my life and being left to raise our four children alone. It all felt so overwhelming. It is overwhelming.

But in the midst of my storm, when it seemed like I could take no more, God whispered a remembrance to me, "My grace is all you need. My power works best in weakness" (2 Corinthians 12:9 NLT). As I clung to that promise, I felt as if my life jacket upgraded to a life raft. I was safe in a boat with a paddle. I still had no real direction, but in surrendering my struggle to God, I felt Him nudging me in certain directions. There is such hope and peace knowing that His power is working best in my broken life as I rely on Him to get me to the next place I need to go in life.

If you are feeling shipwrecked in your life today, I urge you to pray, asking God to give you His power in your weakness and to trust in His grace. He is all you need for today!

Prayer: *Lord*, You see the brokenness of my life. Please be the strength in my weakness, and give me Your grace for today.

Perspective: I understand that widowhood is not for the faint of heart. Though it is an overwhelming journey with feelings of drowning in the ocean, God is a safe lifeboat for our desperate situation.

Prompt: I described my widowhood as feeling shipwrecked. Does that resonate with you? If not, how would you describe your widowhood? What is your life vest? If it is Jesus, how do you see His grace in your life? If it's something other than Jesus, will it truly be enough to hold you in your weakness? What do you need to do to trust God in your brokenness?

4

Fog
(Sharon)

Whoever dwells in the shelter of the Most High
will rest in the shadow of the Almighty.
I will say of the Lord, "He is my refuge
and my fortress, my God, in whom I trust"...
He will cover you with his feathers,
and under his wings you will find refuge;
his faithfulness will be your shield
and rampart
Psalm 91:1–2, 4 NIV

I felt lost in my grief as if a blanket of fog had covered my mind. I had never heard of "widow's fog" before losing Don, but during the first days and months after my husband's death, my thoughts were scattered. I found it hard to make decisions. Everything seemed overwhelming.

In talking with other widows, they too experienced widow's fog. I am convinced that this fog was a gift from the Lord to shield my broken, hurting heart in the very early months of Don's passing. God's grace for the widow is that the fog slowly lifts with time.

During those blurry days, I found God's strength in the beautiful words of Psalm 91. It is an invitation to run into the secret place of the Most High and rest under His shadow. A shadow pictures care and protection from harm, like a mother bird shelters her baby chicks (v. 4). When the fog was so heavy, I snuggled under the shadow and wings of God, feeling His peace, protection, and comfort.

Fog

Prayer: *Heavenly Father,* I run to You for help. In Your gracious love, cover me with Your mighty wings of protection, giving me Your comfort and peace during these difficult days of fog.

Perspective: God will cover you, precious widow, even when your mind is clouded in pain and grief.

Prompt: Have you experienced the "widow's fog"? Journal about how God covered you in those early days of grief.

5

Grief

(Lori)

Guide me in your truth and teach me,
for you are God my Savior, and
my hope is in you all day long.
Psalm 25:5 NIV

I was scrolling through some Instagram posts about grief when I noticed the sculpture *Mélancolie*, by artist Albert György, who is from Geneva. Instantly moved, I studied the sculpture for a long while. A solitary man sat on a bench, his head bowed and shoulders slumped. His posture immediately communicated pain and defeat. He had no face (typical of Geneva sculptures), but that was not what drew me to this particular piece. What spoke to me was the fact that this sad, defeated man had no core. From the shoulders to the waist is a giant gaping hole through which you can see the beautiful landscape behind him.

I resonated with this man because it was like I was looking in the mirror.

After my husband died, my heart hurt. Not my metaphorical heart, but my actual heart that beats inside my chest. My heartbeat would wake me up at night and cause me anxiety during the day. I would constantly hear it in my ears and feel it beating in my chest, making me feel uncomfortable. It reminded me of the story "The Tell-Tale Heart," by Edgar Alan Poe—only I could hear it, my secret, miserable companion keeping me company day and night. My doctor sent me to a cardiologist, who put me through all sorts of tests and monitoring. My actual organ was fine, but I was suffering from a broken heart. My soul had a giant gaping hole in it.

Over the years, I have found that the ache in my heart is still there, but knowing and trusting God has lessened the giant hole in my heart. As Psalm 25:5 (NIV) says, "My hope is in you all day long." When I consciously ask and allow God *to* guide, teach, and heal me, the ache in my heart lessens. I remember that He is the source of hope and life. I am able to breathe better and live more joyfully and freely. The hole in your heart that your husband left behind is deep, dear widow, but God sees it and wants to fill it.

Prayer: God, thank You for seeing our broken hearts and for filling us with the hope we need.

Perspective: The loss of a spouse is so great that it can affect us mentally, physically, emotionally, and spiritually. And yet the hope we have in Jesus can fill us with peace and bring freedom from the anxiety we face.

Prompt: Do you feel like there is a hole missing from the core of your life? Does it keep you in an anxious state? Write down how you are feeling, then write the end of Psalm 25:5 (NIV), "My hope is in you all day long," and pray those words back to Jesus, asking Him to be your hope all through the day.

6
Change

(Sharon)

*For I know the plans I have for you, declares
the Lord, plans to prosper you and not to harm
you, plans to give you hope and a future.*
Jeremiah 29:11 NIV

There was just no way I could prepare myself for the
loss of my husband. I had walked hand in hand with
him, raising our four children, pastoring three churches,
and traveling to many parts of the world doing mission
work—a life truly filled with great adventure as we served
the Lord together.

Now I am alone. *How would I navigate being alone?* is
the question I continued to ask myself. Everything in my
life had changed. My calendar changed, my checkbook
changed, friends changed, where I sat in church changed,
and the list continued to grow. Even where I do my early

morning quiet time had changed. I have cocooned in my bedroom, perhaps because that's where I feel closest to Don. I seem to feel safe and secure there.

No matter how much I wish life didn't change, it *does* change. I now choose to be confident with the new life changes and confident in my God who never changes. Jeremiah 29:11 was written to people who had been taken into captivity. Their lives had changed. They weren't living the lives they had envisioned. Jeremiah wrote about the Lord's plans for their lives, not to harm them but to give them a future and a hope. In fact, they were instructed to grow in the foreign land where they lived.

Life rarely goes according to our plans. Losing a spouse changes our lives. It is not God's plan, however, that we wither away, but His desire is for us to trust Him in the dark time. It's a day-by-day and sometimes hour-by-hour trust in God who never changes as we trust His plan to give us hope and a future.

Change

Prayer: *Heavenly Father*, thank You for never changing. I ask You to give me confidence to walk in Your strength and hope with the new changes in my life.

***

Perspective: We know that this life can change in a moment, and as widows, we have all felt this change. The good news is that God never changes, and what He has promised to you, He will do.

***

Prompt: Even though you aren't living the life you envisioned, God promises hope for your future. But, just like God said to the Israelites, they needed to grow. What has God been putting on your heart recently that you need to do in order to grow? If you can't think of anything, take some time to pray and see if God doesn't bring something to your mind. Then write a prayer to God asking Him to help you take the necessary steps to move forward. Remember, He has a plan for your life and wants to infuse you with hope for a future.

7

Fear

(Lori)

When I am afraid,
I will put my trust in you.
Psalm 56:3 NLT

I never knew I could be so afraid of things until I became a widow. But after my husband died, I became fearful of just about everything. I was afraid of how to spend my money, afraid of raising our kids alone, afraid of being unhealthy for my kids, afraid of having them lose their last parent, and on and on.

Difficulty in life doesn't stop because you are a widow. My fears intensified as my kids went through gut-wrenching struggles, the cars broke down, which cost me more money than I had planned on spending, the house started falling apart, and college tuitions loomed in the future. I would lay in bed at night, thinking of all the things that were out of control in my life, and feel so afraid.

My son, who was struggling with some mental health issues during this time, reached out to a woman in my church who had similar struggles. She told him to find Scripture and memorize it as a tool to battle the inner voices. I thought that was genius, so I adopted the idea. I knew I needed a short verse that would stick easily in my mind.

God led me to Psalm 56:3. This verse has become a mantra in my mind, always arriving when I need it. When I can't sleep at night due to worry: "When I am afraid, I will put my trust in you." When the kids were making hard or unwise decisions: "When I am afraid, I will put my trust in you." When I didn't know where the money was going to come from: "When I am afraid, I will put my trust in you."

Dear widow, God is *for* you! He sees you, knows what makes you afraid, and has a plan for helping you. It may not be the plan you want, but trust Him to lead and guide you in the right direction.

Prayer: *Lord*, help us to trust You instead of our fears, and help us to cling to Your Word for direction and hope.

Perspective: Life is scary and even scarier when you are on your own, making decisions without your spouse. Ask God to lead you to a verse (or use mine) that you can say and pray as a reminder that God is with you and for you.

Prompt: What are you holding in fear about your life today? Pray and surrender them to God and write them down. Make sure to come back and add how God took care of each of these fears!

8

Thankfulness

(Sharon)

Rejoice always; pray continually;
give thanks in all circumstances,
for this is God's will for you in Christ Jesus.
1 Thessalonians 5:16–18 NIV

Hanging on my wall across from my kitchen counter is a large framed picture with this Scripture from 1 Thessalonians, written in beautiful calligraphy. With tears streaming down my face, I have stood in my kitchen, my heart crying out to the Lord, "How can I ever be happy again? How can I give thanks now that I am a widow?"

A few months into my new journey, I felt God gave me two words to stand on: thankfulness and trust. As if He were saying to me, "I know where you are and what you are walking through, and I want you to trust Me and be thankful." It's not easy to do this! There were days that I purposely walked around my home, declaring out loud through tears all I had to be thankful for. I would proclaim in my now quiet house that I *would* trust God. Somehow this practice began to quiet my heart and give me hope.

Even before my deep loss, life has often given me seasons of difficulty where I don't clearly see what God is doing. I know if I choose bitterness and anger, I will miss God's gracious closeness and comfort. I know when I choose to trust my almighty God—when I want Him more than I want answers—that His healing begins to happen. He gives me His joy, not in my circumstances but in Him.

Isaiah 40:31 says, "But they who wait for the Lord shall renew their strength; they shall mount up with wings like eagles; they shall run and not be weary; they shall walk and not faint." I think of the eagle wings as thankfulness and trust. If one of the wings is broken, I won't fly. I need both in my life to strengthen me as I journey through widowhood, the hardest season of my life.

Prayer: *Heavenly Father,* You are such a wonderful, gracious God of comfort and strength. Please help us to lean hard on You and fill our broken hearts with thankfulness and trust.

Perspective: Putting our hope in God and relying on Him will deeply strengthen us. If we use thankfulness and trust as pillars in our lives, just as an eagle uses its wings to propel itself into the sky, we can soar above the bitterness and anger that wants to overtake us.

Prompt: Take a deep cleansing breath. Think about an eagle gliding over the water, stretching its powerful wings. Are you using thankfulness and trust as the two pillars of strength in your life? Using the phrases, "I am thankful for _____ " and "I will trust God with _____," write on sticky notes things that you are thankful for in your life and areas in which you are going to trust God in your life. After writing them out, say them out loud as you read over the phrases. Then put the sticky notes where you will see them around your house.

9

Desperation

(Lori)

*She had heard the reports about Jesus
and came up behind him in the crowd
and touched his garment. For she said,
"If I touch even his garments, I will be made well."*
Mark 5:27–28

When first becoming a widow, I think it's okay to identify yourself as desperate. I know I have been desperate! I once did a message for a women's conference about the woman in Mark chapter 5. She is just described as a woman who had been bleeding for twelve years. Twelve years! In that culture, she wouldn't have been welcomed in anyone's home. She wouldn't be able to get married, and had she been married, her husband could've divorced her. She was a pariah, and she was desperate.

I identify with this woman so much. I don't have a medical issue, but it sure feels like I'm oozing my life blood out of my body. I can't think, I don't want to make decisions, and I just want the pain to go away. But like this woman, I've heard things about Jesus. I've heard He makes blind eyes see and lame people walk. I've heard He can even help the brokenhearted. Mark 5:27–28 (NIV) "She had heard the reports about Jesus and came up behind him in the crowd and touched his garment. For she said, 'If I touch his garments, I will be made well.'" This is an act of desperation.

Of course, after she touches Jesus, she *is* made well. Jesus finds her and tells her, "Daughter, your faith has made you well; go in peace, and be healed of your disease" This woman is brilliant! She went to the only source who could truly heal her. And it's the same source that can help heal you and me.

Dear widow, are you desperate today? Do you feel as if you will never be the same, never fit where you once belonged? There is healing power in knowing Jesus and reaching out for a simple touch from Him. Your pain will probably not miraculously go away; after all, He is teaching you something in the midst of your pain. But He will bring peace and inner strength that you have never felt before. All you have to do is reach out to Him.

Prayer: *Lord*, please be with us desperate widows. We need Your healing touch in the midst of our chaos. Please relieve the pain and guide us in our steps today.

Perspective: If you are feeling desperate, you are not alone! As widows, I think there are things we all experience, and this is one of them. It's not feeling desperate that is the problem—it's what you do with that feeling. Choose to cling to Jesus today, and ask Him to heal your broken heart.

Prompt: In what ways are you feeling desperate today? Is it in the area of sadness, anger, desolation? Read through this story in Mark 5:21–43, and then write your grievances to the Lord because He can handle it! Desperation can make us seek things like alcohol, drugs, or sleep to numb our pain. Go to Him instead!

10

Seasons

(Sharon)

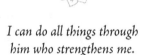

I can do all things through
him who strengthens me.
Philippians 4:13

When I reflect back on the many seasons of life I have walked through as wife, mother, grandmother, and now great-grandmother, each season was unknown before I entered it. I loved each season. My husband and I were enjoying the season of retirement when we received the devasting news of his disease. Now I find myself in a new season called widowhood. It was the one season I never wanted to know.

In this season of being alone, I often feel insecure and scattered. Many times I have stood in my home and cried out loud, "Jesus, help me." Don always handled our finances, paid our bills, knew when the oil should be changed in the car, the tires rotated, and the car filled with gasoline. How would I learn to do all these necessary things that Don did? How would I learn all I needed to know?

I began looking at Philippians 4:13 in a new way: "I can do all [seasons] through him who strengthens me." Yes, God says He is stronger than any season or circumstance that I face. When I don't know who I am or what I should do next, I can trust the One who promises to give me strength for the next step in this new season of widowhood. As I lean on Jesus and trust Him with this truth, this is His promise to help and strengthen me.

Prayer: *Heavenly Father,* in my fears and insecurities, help me to trust You and remember that You will give me the strength I need for every season and circumstance.

Perspective: Widowhood is not a season any of us wanted to take part in, and yet here we are in this sisterhood, together. This is a season that will last the rest of our lives, and yet it is this season that will shape us so much.

Prompt: Write down what you are most struggling with in this new season. Are you willing to trust God in this season as He shapes you into a new mold? Ask God to give you the strength and determination to embrace this new season as He creates something new in you.

11

Why

(Lori)

My soul is very sorrowful, even to death; . . .
My Father, if it be possible, let this cup pass from
me; nevertheless, not as I will, but as you will.
Matthew 26:38–39

I have probably asked God this simple yet complex set of questions a million times: Why? Why did You allow this to happen? Why did You leave me as a single parent? Why didn't You answer our prayers for healing? Why, why, why?

On a basic level, I know why. The Bible tells us that when sin entered into the world, so did death. Death claims a hundred percent of its victims. Even the people Jesus healed and brought back to life eventually died.

Asking this question and looking through the Bible for answers brought me to the Garden of Gethsemane.

Jesus struggled in the face of death too. He entreated His Father in Matthew 26:38–39 to let the cup of death pass from Him.

But it was the will of the Father for His Son to die. There was a greater purpose. Jesus had to die so we could have forgiveness from our sins and spend eternity in heaven. We don't have to know the why of what God is doing in our lives. We only need to submit to His will, knowing that He has a perfect plan.

Following Jesus's example, it is okay to beg God for answers when we are faced with our "why" questions. But when we can't understand, we still need to trust God, knowing that He is faithful and will work all things for the good of those who love Him.

Why

Prayer: Lord, though we don't understand why we are widows, we trust Your will, just like Your Son did, knowing that You have a plan and a purpose for our loss. Give us peace about the questions in our hearts.

Perspective: Jesus knew grief just like we do. He asked God not to make Him go through it, but in the end, He prayed that God's will be done. We can ask God all our why questions, but at the end of the day, God's will is going to be the best. Are we willing to trust what God is doing, or will we live in bitterness toward Him?

Prompt: Read through Matthew 26 to get a good understanding of Jesus's suffering. It wasn't mild. It was so profound that He sweated blood! How are you willing to humble yourself before the Lord and trust His will for your life? Write down whatever answer you choose, and explain to Him why you are responding that way.

12

Anxiety
(Sharon)

*Cast all your anxiety on him
because he cares for you.*
1 Peter 5:7 NIV

After Don died, I felt anxious about so many un-
knowns. The life I had loved for so many years
had instantly changed. I was utterly overwhelmed, and
decisions were hard to make as I began to navigate this
new life alone. Other widows who were further down the
road than I was shared that they had felt the same way.

My husband handled paying our bills, preparing taxes, car repairs, making sure the water softener had salt,
and the list continues to grow. I was responsible now!
Not only was I having to adjust to life without my husband, but I was also learning how to do everything he
had always taken care of.

Fortunately, my son has helped me make a new budget, figure out my taxes, and buy new tires for the car. He even puts salt in the water softener. I am finding that as I do a little each day, God is giving me just what I need to make the next decision. It's kind of like learning to walk again, putting one step in front of the other and slowly moving forward.

There is a Scripture I love that contains some of the most beautiful words ever written. It says, "Cast [give] all your anxiety [worries and cares] on God because He cares for you." It doesn't say to cast a few of my worries on Him, but to cast *all* my insecurities and anxieties on Him. He has unlimited power to comfort, strengthen, and encourage my broken heart. He says to bring *all* to Him, to let go, fall into His loving arms, and trust Him because He cares for me. That's God's love.

Prayer: *Heavenly Father*, show me how to let go of fear and anxiety. Help me to trust and rest in You, knowing You care for me.

Perspective: God cares for you, even in the smallest, most mundane areas of your life. But you need to allow Him in to put His extra on your ordinary.

Prompt: Write your anxieties down on this journal page. Pray and ask God to carry these burdens for you. Here is an exercise for you: Every time you find yourself worrying about one of your worries, come and pick up this book. The action of picking up the book is a physical representation of what you are doing when you take your worries that you just gave over to God and put them back in your own hands. Carry this book around with you until you are ready to pray and set the book down, releasing those worries completely to God. Then watch how He takes care of you.

13

Peace

(Lori)

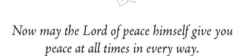

Now may the Lord of peace himself give you
peace at all times in every way.
2 Thessalonians 3:16

*T*rying to fit the words "widow" and "peaceful" in the same sentence can be a challenge. For me, I can sometimes feel anything but peaceful! When I think of being at peace and in a peaceful state of mind, I imagine myself lying by a pool overlooking the ocean, enjoying a good book and a cold drink. Or taking a hike on a gorgeous Colorado trail in the cool of the morning, watching the sun appear on the horizon. Neither of these illustrations would I use to describe what it's like to be a widow.

Second Thessalonians 3:16 says, "Now may the Lord of peace himself give you peace at all times in every way."

Did you know that another name for Jesus is the Prince of Peace? In other words, Jesus *is* peace, and you can *know* peace by knowing Him.

What does this mean when we are experiencing loss? Loss tends to feel uncertain, hopeless, and restless. Peace feels certain, hopeful, and content. The second part of that verse says that God can give you peace at all times and in every way. God wants us to be at peace in our innermost being even when our life's circumstances are seemingly out of control.

The key to knowing peace in our lives is knowing God. If you have never asked God into your life, take a minute to invite Him in. We then need to pray to the source of peace and ask Him to fill us with His comfort, to lead us as we walk in His will for our lives so that we can truly know peace and contentment.

Prayer: Lord, give us the peace we need to live our lives with certainty, a hope for the future, and contentment in our now.

Perspective: To truly know peace, we need to know the Prince of Peace who can give us peace at all times in every way.

Prompt: Take some time and really contemplate if you have made that decision to accept Jesus into your heart and life. In the back of this book, there is an explanation of what it means to surrender your life to the Prince of Peace and how to do it. If you have already made that decision, then take some time to search your heart and see if there is anything you are struggling with to find peace. In this journaling space, write your struggles to the One who is peace and ask Him to fill you with abundant peace.

14

Treasures

(Sharon)

*I will give you the treasures of darkness, And
hidden wealth of secret places,
So that you may know that it is I,
The Lord, the God of Israel,
who calls you by your name.*
Isaiah 45:3 NASB

Grief is a time of darkness and loneliness. When I first read this verse from Isaiah, I was taken aback. How can there be treasures in darkness? Stumbling through the early, deep, dark months of grief, continuously crying and feeling alone and lost, the hope of treasures eluded me.

My husband and I had the privilege of doing mission work overseas. One summer, on a ministry trip to the Czech Republic, we had meetings in a beautiful spa city named Kalavory Vary. A river flowed through the middle of the town. On each side of the town were colonnades (long sidewalks with column structures supported by a roof) with shops and bakeries.

The beautiful mountain spa town was known for its many hot springs of healing mineral waters. People would travel miles to relax, drink the mineral waters, and bask in the waters. It was so fascinating to watch as people walked the colonnades, drinking from beautiful porcelain cups with sipping spouts. We were told minerals in the water from these deep wells would help people with indigestion and other stomach issues, even joint and back pain.

These healing waters remind me of God's Word. It contains treasures of healing for my broken, thirsty heart. In my grief, God has been faithful to give me a little taste of encouragement and hope as I sip on the "hidden wealth" found in His Word. When my grief has taken me into deep darkness, I drink deep of this truth: the Word of God is mine to treasure, and the God who wrote it knows my name.

Prayer: Heavenly Father, we are so thankful You have deep, healing treasures in the Bible. You know our names, and You lavishly give us treasures of wealth in our darkest hours.

Perspective: Just like there are mineral waters that heal the body, the Word of God can heal our souls of the damage from loss and grief.

Prompt: Need a good book of the Bible to jump into? I would recommend any of the Gospels, but I particularly like the book of John. The study of Jesus's life is amazing, and we can learn so many things through Him. Read a chapter today and journal what stuck out to you. If you already have a reading plan, journal here what God is teaching you.

15

Holidays
(Lori)

Look to the Lord and his strength;
seek his face always.
1 Chronicles 16:11 NIV

The holiday seasons hold so many emotions as a widow.
These emotions are intensified by having children in
the house. You want to make the holidays special, but pulling out all the traditional things can be a punch to the gut.

Thanksgiving had always been my family's big celebration day. We would go to the grandparents' house early in the week and start decorating for Christmas. Each child had their own specific piece of Christmas to set up, and they loved being a part of the traditions. Usually the night before Thanksgiving, we would spend the night, and the kids would watch movies with their dad and Papa while my mom and I would cook in the kitchen. It was wonderful and magical. The sound of mixers twirling, children laughing, timers beeping, and the smell of cookies baking are treasured memories.

But that year, Thanksgiving—*the* treasured holiday— was a terrible experience. My husband went into a hospice facility during the month of November and was there for five weeks until he passed on December 6. We spent Thanksgiving eating grilled cheese that some sweet man, who had had a loved one once in the hospice facility, graciously made for the people in the care center. My husband, the shopaholic that he was, had purchased these beautiful Thanksgiving tablecloths earlier in the year. They were incredible, and I had been looking forward to using them. We ended up letting our extended family use them, and ever since then, I have stored the tablecloths in my linen closet.

Every widow is different. Some widows love to use all the traditional things, making them feel like their spouse is close, while others don't need the reminder because it causes pain. My encouragement to you, widow, is to take a deep breath and think about what feels good to you. If having all the remembrances of your spouse around your house feels comforting, do that. If not having anything the same and changing up everything for you and your family feels more peaceful, then do that.

However, don't compare! We tend to think that because someone did it differently, that person is clearly the better widow. My mom and I have experienced so many of the same feelings, but we each have had to grieve in our own ways.

Something that has helped me get through holidays and anniversaries with joy is to prepare for them. When the calendar pages show a date is fast approaching, I gear myself up, and then for my kids' sake, I decide beforehand to be happy that day. Although I know the loss will be felt by all of us, I choose to enter the day determined to make it new and special.

And I always pray. Our verse today tells us where to look for strength. God is always there for you, and together, you can face the day. Let's seek the face of the Lord when we are faced with hard anniversaries and holidays.

Prayer: Lord, give us the strength we need to get through the tough days and to do it with anticipation for how You are going to make it special.

Perspective: There is no right or wrong way to celebrate a holiday after your spouse is gone. Give yourself space for something new, and never compare yourself to someone else.

Prompt: Is there a holiday or anniversary coming up? Take a moment to sit and think about what feels right to do this year. Write down some traditions you want to keep and something new you can try.

16

Hands

(Sharon)

For I am the Lord your God
who takes hold of your right hand
and says to you, Do not fear; I will help you.
Isaiah 41:13 NIV

*H*olding hands was something Don and I enjoyed. Today on my morning walk, I felt of wave of sadness wash over me as I was missing Don walking by my side and holding my hand. We often would walk together in the mornings through our neighborhood, holding hands, talking and praying together for our family. I felt loved and protected when I held his hand. Sometimes, like this morning, grief took me by surprise. I would give anything to hold my precious husband's hand again.

I've learned that when this happens, it's okay to ponder over these sweet memories and allow tears to arise.

I've heard it said that "when you love deeply, you grieve deeply."

God's Word talks many times about the strong hand of God, stretched out to help and bring comfort. In Isaiah 41:13, it says that I don't have to fear because God is there to hold my hand. His hand is in mine when I'm missing my husband's hand. It's such a comfort to know that when I falter and am afraid on my new journey of widowhood, I can hold tight to His understanding hand. He promises to hold my hand tightly and help me.

Hands

Prayer: *Heavenly Father* . . . I miss holding my husband's hand. This new journey is hard. Please hold my hand and cover me with Your tender love and comfort.

Perspective: The little things mean so much. Holding hands is just one of many things we grieve the loss of after our spouse is gone. The amazing thing is that God is willing to help and comfort us as we grieve.

Prompt: What small things are you grieving that you did with your spouse? Take some time and write a special memory of doing that with your spouse. What a gift memories are! Choose to thank God for the time you had with your spouse, creating memories instead of focusing on the loss. Then ask God to comfort you and help you today.

17
Guilt
(Lori)

*You keep him in perfect peace whose mind is
stayed on you, because he trusts in you. Trust
in the Lord forever, for the Lord God is an
everlasting rock.*
Isaiah 26:3–4

Being my husband's caregiver meant helping him stay
alive for as long as possible. I didn't let myself sleep
deeply for two years. My husband had a neurological disease
called MSA, which is a kissing cousin to ALS. For two years,
I had to feed him, bathe him, clothe him, and translate his
speech so people could understand what he was saying.

When the day came that the doctors told me there was
nothing more that could be done for him, I took them at
their word and put him into hospice. It took five long weeks
for him to pass away. During those weeks, I was already feeling the guilt of giving up on keeping him alive. I asked him
if he was tired of fighting to stay alive, and he said no. His
answer was not what I wanted to hear. I wanted him to agree

with me (who was exhausted from the fight) and say that it was time to be tired. He did gracefully give up the fight and agree with the doctors, family, and myself that nothing more could be done, but that did nothing to alleviate my guilt of feeling like I gave up when he was still in the fight.

Since then, I have these guilty feelings that pop up every so often. Even my dreams haunt me, making me feel guilty, as if I didn't do enough for my husband. Should I have fought longer with him? What if I gave up on him too soon? What if there was a cure around the corner? What if, what if, what if? In my most vulnerable moments, I am tempted to berate and second guess myself and let my guilt eat away at me.

It was a few years after Greg died that I was speaking about my guilt to my sister. She asked me a great question that really had me searching my heart: "Did you do the best you could with the knowledge you possessed at the time?" I had. I tried my best. "Well then," she said, "what more was there to do? Can you trust that God guided you, our family, and the doctors to the best decisions? Can you leave your guilt behind and trust God's plan?"

As I wrestled with questioning if I could trust God and that He guided our paths, God led me to Isaiah 26:3–4. "You keep him in perfect peace whose mind is stayed on you, because he trusts in you. Trust in the lord forever, for the lord God is an everlasting rock." I prayed a million times that God would heal my husband and guide us to the best possible solutions. I know He heard our prayers.

I need to let go of the guilt and cling to the promise of God—to remind myself that even if there was something else I could have done to help Greg stay alive, today he is in the midst of God and the glories of heaven! He wouldn't choose to stay a day longer or come back if he had the chance! I need to recognize the hard work I put into helping him and remember that I did everything I could. I need to forgive myself of the "what ifs?" and remind myself that God is in control.

Prayer: Lord, please take the guilt away from me today and help me to walk in freedom.

Perspective: Do you struggle with guilt? Maybe it's over the things you said to your spouse, or maybe it's what you didn't say. Death is so final, and we can guilt ourselves over the should haves, would haves, and could haves. If this is something you are struggling with, let today be the day that you release it.

Prompt: In this journal space, write what you are feeling guilty about. Once it's written down, pray that God would forgive you and release you from your guilt. Then ask Him for some tangible ways you can do this and write that, down. Every time you go back to guilting yourself, come back here and remind yourself that you are forgiven and can live in freedom and with peace.

18

Trust

(Sharon)

*Trust in the Lord with all your heart
and lean not on your own understanding;
in all your ways acknowledge him,
and he will make your paths straight.*
Proverbs 3:5–6 NIV

I don't get to choose my life story. If I could, I would choose an easy life. Each day would be filled with sunshine, fun, and joy. There would be only happy endings for myself and everyone I love. Widowhood definitely wouldn't have been written into my story. But it isn't my story to write.

The truth is, no one gets to choose the easy life. Life is filled not only with sunshine, fun, and joy but also with clouds, rain, and wind. On my walk this morning, clouds were on the horizon, and by evening, storms will begin to blow across the skies. Widowhood is like a storm. It can come on slowly, or it can hit quickly. In the storm of widowhood, I am learning to trust and hang on to the One who is with me in the storm.

Think of it! The Lord God who formed and made the universe is my God! He sees my fragile heart, holds my shaking hand, and says, "Trust me." He urges me to lean hard on Him, and when I do, His promise is to make my difficult path straight. I can trust that if I could see what He sees, I would say, "Yes, Lord! I may not be able to choose my story, but I can choose to trust You. With You, I know I will be safe in this storm."

Prayer: *Heavenly Father*, I confess this part of my story is so hard. I am choosing to trust You to help me through this storm of widowhood.

Perspective: Widowhood is a scary life storm. The good news is that we know the One who can lead us through it in the midst of its intensity.

Prompt: I love the song "Oceans" by Hillsong. It talks about how Peter walked on the water in the midst of a storm. However, when he took his eye off Jesus, that is when he began to sink. We will do the same thing in our lives if we don't place our trust in Him. Listen to this song, and then write a prayer to God, telling Him that you will trust Him to write you the best story for your life, even with the storms.

19

Broken

(Lori)

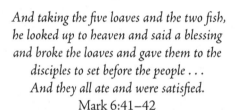

And taking the five loaves and the two fish,
he looked up to heaven and said a blessing
and broke the loaves and gave them to the
disciples to set before the people . . .
And they all ate and were satisfied.
Mark 6:41–42

I love looking at broken glass mosaics. Somehow the artists take something that is broken, and what others may just throw away, and use the broken pieces to put it together in a new and beautiful way! As a widow, I look at my life as a mosaic piece of art. My life had once been whole and such a beautiful picture but now has been shattered into a million pieces. As I am trying to put these broken shards back together, I often long for that original piece of art. But it will never look the same. I am finding beauty in the brokenness and in the way my new life is taking shape.

A well-known Bible story displays a miracle after Jesus breaks something. In Mark 6:41–42, Jesus took the bread and fish that were whole, blessed it, then broke it and used it to create a miracle to feed five thousand people. You may feel like broken bread or scattered pieces of fish, but in the hands of Jesus, you are a miracle in the making!

I know the breaking is not fun. Think of how messy breaking bread and fish was for Jesus! But the end result was a miracle. When you give your life over to God's will, even when He gives and takes away, you are allowing Him to do a miracle in your life. There is blessing in the process of breaking. I know how badly it hurts, but hold on to Jesus and wait for Him to put your pieces back together. He will do it in His timing and in a way you would never know could be so beautiful. God wants to use your brokenness to bless you and others around you.

Prayer: *Lord*, take our broken pieces and do what only You can do. Bless us in the breaking and make a miracle out of our lives.

Perspective: There's a blessing in the midst of your brokenness. God will take your broken pieces and orchestrate them in a new and beautiful way.

Prompt: Honest answer required here: Are you allowing God to do a miracle in your broken life? Or are you resentful at how your life is going and unwilling to let Him put your pieces back together? In this journal space, write to God, asking Him to help you allow the miracle of being broken become a blessing in your life.

20

Traditions

(Sharon)

Blessed be the God and Father of our Lord Je-
sus Christ, the Father of mercies and God of all
comfort, who comforts us in all our affliction so
that we may be able to comfort those who are
in any affliction with the comfort with which
we ourselves are comforted by God.
2 Corinthians 1:3–4 NASB

God showed up . . . like big time showed up. Four
months after Don passed away, it was Christmas.
My choice would have been to bypass Christmas, but our
family wanted to be together and at my home with all
the traditional foods such as Christmas punch, brisket,
shrimp, cheese balls, and oyster stew. Don loved Christmas, and he was always in charge of reading the Bible
story, then supervising the orderly handing out of gifts
one by one. I had prayed all day while I prepared food for

the evening, asking God to please hold my heart strong and give me the right words to share with my family this first Christmas.

All of a sudden, while most were still eating, there was laughter. We could hear wrapping paper ripping in the great room. One cute great-grandchild decided he couldn't wait to open his gift. Other little ones jumped in on the fun, and soon, we all joined with gifts flying through the air and joy filling the room! This was a Christmas unlike any we had ever experienced, but we all agreed it was exactly the Christmas we needed.

Later, as I reflected on the wonderful evening, I thought about this verse which says our God is "the Father of mercies and God of all comfort, who comforts us in all our afflictions." 2 Corinthians 1:3–4 (NASB) What I was dreading, God enveloped my home and brought His comfort, leaving us with a Christmas to always remember.

Prayer: *Heavenly Father*, thank You for being a God who provides your mercies and comfort knowing just what we need when our hearts are filled with sorrow and missing our loved one.

Perspective: Our God is a Father of all mercies and comfort, and He tenderly watches over our every need.

Prompt: As widows, there are days we know will be difficult, and perhaps we are dreading them. In this journal space, write these difficult days down. Ask God to show up and comfort you in ways that you never imagined. Make sure to come back and document what God did for you this day. It's no guarantee that these hard days will be wonderful, so come back and document, even if it didn't turn out how you expected. Search your heart, and God will give you the comfort you need!

21

Sorrow

(Lori)

Jesus wept.
John 11:35

*L*et's get real here. When it comes to crying, not all tears are equal. In my dreams, I would look like Demi Moore did in the movie, *Ghost*, when she cried after losing the love of her life. The scene is almost magical. The camera does a close up of her, and you can see her flushed face take on an expression of awe, her mouth opening slightly. Her eyes fill with unshed tears, and we wait with bated breath for what is about to happen. Then slowly, dramatically, with the hauntingly sorrowful notes of "Unchained Melody" playing softly in the background, her big, fat, beautiful tears fall slowly from her slightly reddened eyes.

In reality, however, my eyes swell, my nose gets Rudolph red, cheeks turn blotchy like I have rosacea, and liquids start running. This is what grieving looks like. It's not pretty or camera worthy. It comes from a desperate soul in anguish. And yet, despite the ugliness that greets me in the mirror, there is beauty to my tears. Those tears *mean* something. They are special—they are important. They are shed for me, my kids, my family, my future. I spent a long time with those tears, and I am beyond grateful that they matter to God as well (Psalm 56:8).

The shortest verse in Scripture is probably one of the most impactful verses as well. John 11:35 says, "Jesus wept." Jesus felt the sting of tears over the loss of a close friend and, while it wasn't over a spouse, Jesus can still identify with the loss we are experiencing. How amazing is it that your Savior can identify with those precious tears you and your family shed? The God who created you and loves you the most and knows you the best can not only empathize with you but can also comfort you in your sorrow.

Prayer: *Lord*, thank You for not just knowing about our loss, but for experiencing it Yourself. Comfort us in our grieving and guide us in our next steps in life.

Perspective: Tears are a reality of being a widow. They are precious, and even Jesus wept in grief. He knows what it is like to feel grief, and we can trust Him with our own. Ask Him to give you peace, comfort, and direction for your next step.

Prompt: In this journal space, write down what is making you weep today. I know this will be a painful exercise, but there is something healing about putting pen to paper and clearing out all that is in your mind. After you've written what's on your heart, pray for yourself. See yourself as Jesus sees you, and have compassion and understanding for the hurt. Then pray for God to give you wisdom in your next steps forward.

22

Loneliness

(Sharon)

*And my God will meet all your needs
according to to the riches of his glory
in Christ Jesus.*
Philippians 4:19 NIV

Days can be long and lonely as a widow and the home filled with silence, but I am finding God knows exactly what I need. I received a text from my grandson who wanted to know if I was still up. It was late, but he and his dog were out taking a walk, and he wanted to stop by to see me. The evening air was lovely, so I told him to come by. We sat on my back patio, where we chatted amid the light breeze and soft tinkling of the beautiful wind chimes a friend had sent in memory of Don. My heart was refreshed with this short visit.

In the early days of adjusting to being a widow, I found the Lord knew how to give me encouragement and hope. Philippians 4:19 has taken on new meaning for me. Consider Paul, who was suffering in prison and lonely while writing encouraging words about God suppling all our needs according to His glorious riches in Christ Jesus. God's resources were sufficient for Paul's loneliness, and they are sufficient for us too.

Every day in my loneliness, God has graciously provided the strength I need to take just one more step. When I feel alone, God knows just how to encourage me and give me what I need. Like a late-night visit from a grandson and his dog. My God supplies all I need when I lean hard into Him and trust His tender care.

Prayer: Dear Heavenly Father, thank You for this promise to supply whatever need I am walking through with Your glorious riches in Christ Jesus.

Perspective: When we are in communication with God regularly, we can tell Him what we are thinking and feeling. He knows just what we need and can supply it to us at just the right time.

Prompt: Loneliness can make your soul hurt. Use this journal to write to God about the hurt and sorrow you are feeling. Ask God to bring people into your life at just the right time to help you know you are not alone.

23

Love

(Lori)

*How precious is your unfailing love,
O God! All humanity finds
shelter in the shadow of your wings.*
Psalm 36:7 NLT

When Greg started to lose his voice and communicating with him became difficult, we started getting creative on how we could communicate. We started squeezing each other's hands, and we would say, "A squeeze means 'I love you.'" We had no idea how precious this gesture would become to us.

After Greg's brain surgery, we had about three good weeks before the unforeseeable happened. He went into respiratory failure and ended up on life support. As he lay in the ICU with a tube down his throat and so many wires in and around him, I took his nonresponsive hand in mine and squeezed it as if my life depended on it. And while he didn't squeeze back, it didn't matter. My goal was to simply let him know that I was there with him and that I loved him.

Now, as a widow, I feel like I am that lifeless, unresponsive person—numb and looking for someone to squeeze my hand, letting me know that I am loved. This is when I call out to God, telling Him I need something—anything—and I feel a gentle squeeze from my heavenly Father. What does that squeeze look like? It could be an unexpected call from my children. Maybe a friend asks to have coffee with me. Sometimes it's the sermon on Sunday, when my pastor seems to know just what I need to hear. God's love for me knows no bounds. He loved me so much that He sent His Son to die for me! This is the kind of love that truly never fails.

Prayer: *Lord*, please remind me today of how much You love me, and give me a gentle squeeze to let me know that You are with me.

⌢

Perspective: Look at "coincidences" in your life and realize that maybe God is trying to give you a squeeze and remind you how much He loves you.

⌢

Prompt: In this journal space, write down one area in your life where you would like to feel a squeeze from God. Write down a time when you know God was giving a reminder of His love. Then write the name of a person or another widow you know and something you can do in their lives to let them know that God loves them.

24

Sundays
(Sharon)

*The Lord is near to the brokenhearted
and saves the crushed in spirit.
Many are the afflictions of the righteous,
but the Lord delivers him out of them all.*
Psalm 34:18–19

I always loved going to church with my husband every week. It was part of our vocation when Don was a pastor, and I loved watching him preach the Word of God from the pulpit. Once he retired, we walked into the building together faithfully every week, and it was a gift to have him sit next to me. Sundays are hard now, and I'm slowly learning to navigate the empty space.

When Don first passed, I had to decide if I would just stay home or if I would get myself dressed and go to church. The thought of sitting alone in the service was daunting. The Psalms speak often about God's comfort for those who feel most alone. One particular verse has been a solace for me: "The Lord is near to the brokenhearted and saves the crushed in spirit" (Psalm 34:18). Could I trust God with my Sundays, when I was feeling brokenhearted and alone? And as He always does, God gave me grace when I was grieving, and every week, He provided a loving friend or family member to sit with during worship.

At a recent Sunday morning service, the worship pastor sang these familiar lyrics, "When we all get to heaven, what a day of rejoicing that will be." Memories flooded my heart of singing that song with Don by my side. He loved to sing, and I loved hearing him sing. Yes, someday we will again sing together in heaven, praising Him for His wondrous love and care.

Prayer: *Heavenly Father*, thank You that You are so closely attuned to broken hearts, and I can trust You to help me on my hardest days.

Perspective: Routines can be so hard on us widows. They seem to amplify that we are now alone. God says in His Word that He is close to those who are broken-hearted and that He will deliver us from our afflictions.

Prompt: What routines are hard for you? What made them special? Journaling our thoughts and feelings helps us move our pent-up energy onto the paper. I know it's not easy to do, but sometimes you will surprise yourself with how you are really feeling. Tell God about your broken heart and ask Him to deliver you from it.

25

Prayer

(Lori)

*You know when I sit down
and when I rise up;
you discern my thoughts from afar.*
Psalm 139:2

Have you ever heard someone say, "Well, I guess all we can do now is pray," like it's the last resort? As widows, prayer should be our starting point. This is where we go to spiritual battle for ourselves and for others. There is nothing more that the evil one would like us to do than to give up on prayer! But what do you do when you don't feel like praying or don't have any words to say?

There are times when I am too exhausted to pray and times when I feel too angry at God. There are times when I am so overwhelmed that I don't know where to begin my prayer or what to ask for from God.

Even in these times, God is so good to us. In Psalm 139:2, it says, "He discerns our thoughts from afar." God's got you! He knows where you are at this moment, and He knows your needs and desires.

Prayer has helped me so much, but especially when I first became a single mom. I told God straight up, "Okay, God! You allowed my kids' dad to be taken away. Now You need to be their Father and bring other father figures into their lives." I cannot tell you how many ways God has fulfilled this prayer of mine! Sometimes He has answered in ordinary ways, and other times He has answered in ways that can only be described as miraculous.

So where do we begin our prayer? For me, sometimes I lay down on my bed (a skill I have perfected at this point), open my arms wide, look at the ceiling, and just say to God, "Help." Other times I get on my knees by my bed and read my journal where I have written all the areas in my life that need His attention. Whatever your posture, all you have to do is reach out to Him. Remember, He is God and is able to handle whatever you throw at Him. Even in your anger and hurt, He is good and faithful!

Prayer: *Lord*, thank You for knowing right where we are and discerning our thoughts even when we sometimes can't do it for ourselves. Help us to cry out to You every day.

Perspective: Prayer is our battle ground. It's where we go to release our issues and allow God to fight on our behalf. Don't worry if you don't have the words—God knows what's on your heart and just what you need for today.

Prompt: Start a prayer list. This is a list that you can add to. Don't forget to come back and write down how God answered your prayers. This will be invaluable to you when you want to doubt God. All you have to do is come back and read how He carried you through all the other times in your life.

26

Comfort
(Sharon)

For I will turn their mourning to joy,
Will comfort them, And make them
rejoice rather than sorrow.
Jeremiah 31:13 NKJV

I kept churning over in my mind what to do with the clothes closet I had shared with my love for sixty years. I took up the biggest part of the closet during our marriage, but he still had *his* side. Months after Don's passing, my heart would still skip a beat every time I came into the closet. His clothes hanging in his space brought comfort to me. Sometimes I would just stare, tears rolling down my face as I remembered how I loved seeing him in those shirts. Sometimes I hugged his shirts against my cheek, breathing in his smells.

Thankfully, grief sets no timeframe for when to clean out the closet. But as months passed, an idea crept into my mind to make a blanket out of Don's shirts. My precious granddaughter, who is a gifted quilter, jumped on the idea when I presented it to her. When I felt it was time to let go, I gingerly packed his shirts in a bag for her to take to her home for quilting. Now I am comforted with a beautiful quilt, fashioned together with pieces of my husband's shirts. Priceless memories. In addition to the quilt, each family member was gifted a beautifully quilted pillow made from their dad's and papa's shirts.

Yes, we can trust God to turn our mourning into comfort as we navigate through the new days of widowhood. This Scripture reminds us that one day our mourning will be turned to joy. We will be comforted, and we will rejoice rather than sorrow. Be patient with yourself. God is patient with us and never in a hurry. He is filled with compassion and is the God of all comfort. Even with such a simple thing as a blanket made of precious old clothes, God shows us His love and comfort. We can trust Him to bring joy out of sorrow in His time.

Prayer: *Heavenly Father,* walking in widowhood is so hard. I cry out to You to give me Your wisdom about how to make good decisions in the right timing. Thank You for Your comfort and the hope that someday my mourning will turn to joy.

Perspective: Our spouse's "things" can give us both comfort and sorrow. There is no time frame of how long we have to keep them or get rid of them. Maybe repurposing them could be a great way to let go and hang on at the same time.

Prompt: What are the things of your spouse that give you comfort? What are some tangible items you could use to turn into precious memories? Write about what makes them so special. Remembering the good memories can bring comfort during the days of sorrow.

27

Anger

(Lori)

*And so we know and rely on the love God
has for us. God is love. Whoever lives in love
lives in God, and God in them.*
1 John 4:16 NIV

The pain I felt at becoming a widow quickly built up some serious anger inside of me. After all, I had been a good person, served God in my life, and loved my husband deeply. It didn't seem fair that God took not only my husband away but also my ministry, my work, and the father to my children. I had a severe case of the "poor me" syndrome.

There were times when I wanted to ice out God and hold Him at arm's length. When life continued to be difficult and depressing without Him, I finally came to my senses and realized it was best for me to include Him in my mental musings. But I still felt so angry at Him, and I would unleash my rage at Him in our conversations. I was in so much pain and so overwhelmed with this new life and single parenting that I put the blame for all the wrongs in my life squarely at His feet. I accused Him of not being fair and of not loving me. However, this accusation felt wrong because I had heard so many times that God *does* love me. Romans 8:38–39 is a great example, saying that nothing can separate us from the love of God. I had to agree that God does love me, but maybe He doesn't like me very much, and that is why my life hurt so much.

Let me explain. When I was teaching school, of course I loved all my students. But, if I were completely honest, there were some kids that I did not especially like. It was easy to reward the good kids while others made it very difficult. Was I like that unlikeable kid to God?

The Scripture today points out to us that God literally *is* perfected, unconditional love. God is love, and more than that, He loves you and me! He doesn't pick favorites, and He can't like us only a little. There is no way that God loves us less or lets bad things into our lives. Bad things happen in our lives because we live in a fallen world. When sin entered this planet in the lives of Adam and Eve, so did decay, destruction, disease, and every other miserable thing that can happen.

When we doubt God's love for us, we are believing the lie that the evil one wants us to believe. What we really need is perspective. For me, I reread verses about His love for me, remembered His sacrifice on the cross, and then wrote down all the blessings in my life. And while my life may not be perfect, I know He has a plan and purpose for everything that has happened, and He can use my pain to help me and others around me.

If you find yourself battling with anger toward God in your life, let me encourage you. You are not alone! God loves you in the good, bad, and ugly. He truly is the definition of love and wants to make your biggest pain your greatest strength.

Prayer: *Lord*, thank You for being love and for understanding our anger and pain. Please help us to surrender it to You so You can help us to become better instead of bitter.

Perspective: God loves you even when you are out of control with anger toward Him. You can trust Him not to turn His back on you if you rage at Him. He is strong enough for your toughest questions and emotions. Your action step is to draw closer to Him and trust Him in your daily life.

Prompt: What anger are you holding toward God today? Write out your grievances and then write, BUT GOD IS LOVE. Take time to meditate on that. Just like your children think you are unfair to them, we can think God is being unfair to us. But remember how much you love your children, and then imagine being able to have perfect love. Take time to realize that is how God loves you. Now write down some things in your life that let you know of and show you God's love.

28

Memories

(Sharon)

*What shall I return to the Lord for all His
goodness to me? I will lift up the cup of salva-
tion and call on the name of the Lord.*
Psalm 116:12–13 NIV

When I was a young mother, I always enjoyed getting up early before the children or Don began to stir. I treasured the early, quiet mornings and usually had to set my alarm to make it happen. It was my time. Even after the kids moved out and it was just Don and me, I still loved having my early morning quiet time.

I have a favorite chair in my office where I curl up with my cup of coffee, my Bible, books, and a journal. It's my space to read a devotion, pray, journal, and listen to God. These last few years, when Don came from the bedroom, he would join me in my office where we would chat about the day ahead of us. So many good talks and plans were shared together in that office space.

Now the early morning chats are over, but I treasure the memories. I look forward to being with Don in heaven and having those chat times together again. I'm sure they will be filled with gratitude and joy as we remember the wonderful blessings God poured out to us through the years.

I love the Scripture that says, "What shall I return to the Lord for all his goodness to me?" (Psalm 116:12 NIV) David, the psalmist, was looking back and pouring out his heart of thankfulness for all God had given him. Even in my loneliness, I want to remember God's goodness to me with a heart of gratitude. I'm going to take what I have been given and today choose to give God glory.

Prayer: *Heavenly Father*, even as my heart is sad and lonely, I want to be grateful for all You have done for me. Thank You for memories and the future I have to look forward to being together again with my husband.

Perspective: God is good to us, even in the depths of grief. Remembering the good times we had with our spouse can feel so bittersweet, but when we focus on the time that God gave us for those precious memories, we can see His goodness in our lives.

Prompt: Journal a cherished memory you shared with your spouse. Then write a thank you letter to God for the time He gave you together to make those memories.

29

Wisdom

(Lori)

If you need wisdom,
ask our generous God,
and he will give it to you.
James 1:5 NLT

*I*t always seems to happen at night. The busy day that kept my mind away from the grieving and sorrowful thoughts ends, and now it's able to unwind and go to those places I tried so hard to forget during the day. But being a single parent, it's not just my grief that I have to confront and battle. I also have to help my children.

There was no way I could have prepared for this before my husband died. No parent knows what to say the first time their baby girl comes into the bedroom late at night, crying her little heart out because she misses her daddy. The thing is, now that she is a young adult, I still don't have the right words to say.

So I take a deep breath and pray for the wisdom I lack. "God, I need wisdom. You are a generous God. Give me the right words to help my hurting child."

Memories come flooding to my mind: some good, some bad, some funny, some sad. I remind her of her dad's presence in her life. I remind her that he fought so hard to stay alive for her and her brothers, and that he wanted so badly to be here for them. I remind her that he loves her so much and would be so proud of the beautiful young woman she is becoming. I tell her the funny stories she's heard before, and then I tell her some she might not have heard. We laugh together and we cry together. Then I remind her that God, who loves us all more than we can imagine, had a different plan. Though we may never understand, we can trust because He loves us so much.

Being a single parent to grieving children is a staggering responsibility. Fortunately, we have a gracious God who is always there to give us what we need. He doesn't just give the bare minimum but a generous amount of wisdom. All we need to do is ask.

Prayer: Lord, give me the wisdom I need to help my children through what they are experiencing. Help me to know the right words to comfort their hearts.

Perspective: The bond God creates between you and your children after the death of your spouse is priceless. Single mom, I know how tired you are and how overwhelming it can be, but hang in there. Try and look at this time as a treasure and not a burden. Use the grief to pull you closer together and not further apart.

Prompt: It's easy to want to isolate yourself from other people's pain when you have so much of your own. Whether you have children who are young or old, use the grief as a common bond. Write down your own prayer that asks God to give you generous amounts of wisdom to help guide your children and strengthen your relationships.

30

Protection

(Sharon)

*Do not be anxious about anything, but in
every situation, by prayer and petition, with
thanksgiving, present your requests to God.
And the peace of God, which transcends all
understanding, will guard your hearts and
your minds in Christ Jesus.*
Philippians 4:6–7 NIV

Each night before going to bed, Don would check all
the doors and set the home alarm. I never worried
about the doors or security as we slept because I knew
Don made sure the doors were locked. Now it's my job. I
find myself double checking the doors to make sure each
one is locked and the alarm is set.

There are times when fear sneaks into my bedroom
at night, causing me to be afraid. It's lonely crawling into
my empty bed, missing the protection I used to enjoy

when I would snuggle against my husband. I know other widows say they also struggle with fear at night.

Philippians 4:6 (NIV) says, "Do not be anxious about anything." How can I do this? This Scripture gives the secret to not being anxious or fearful. We can call out in prayer and ask for the Lord's protection. Although I lock the doors of my home, I need to lean into Jesus, who is the guard over the door of my heart and mind. When I turn out the light and darkness covers my bedroom, I can rest in His protection. I ask Him to protect my home and allow me to rest in peace. I received a pillowcase which has written on it, "IN HIS PRESENCE, I find rest." Psalm 4:8 says, "In peace I will both lie down and sleep; for you alone, O Lord, make me dwell in safety."

Prayer: *Heavenly Father*, You are a God of love and care for our hearts when they feel fear or are anxious. Please place Your protection not only over our home but also our heart.

Perspective: As a widow, feeling protected can be hard to experience; however, God longs to provide it for us and to comfort us in our anxieties. We need to ask God to fill us with His peace, trusting that He is in control of our lives and there to protect us, even when our lives feel out of control.

Prompt: Do you find yourself afraid at night? Or maybe it's some other time during the day. Write down your fears to God and pray that His peace will fill your heart and life. Pray His protection around you and your family. Try writing Psalm 4:8 and putting it where it will remind you to trust God with your fears.

31

Shepherd

(Lori)

The Lord is my shepherd;
I shall not want.
Psalm 23:1

*R*ight after Greg passed away, I took my boys on a trip to Israel and Turkey with my family. It was a trip their father had taken, so I wanted them to experience what he had experienced. While there, our guide took us to the Mediterranean coast. Gazing at the ocean's power and beauty, one can easily overlook a well-worn statue of a shepherd holding a lamb around his neck. Fortunately for us, our guide pointed this statue out to us.

He began to talk about what it's like to be a shepherd and also about the behavior of sheep. The shepherd's job is one of protection and direction for the sheep who easily lose their way and are prone to get run down by a predator or hurt themselves. Often a sheep will injure itself, and when that happens, it spends six full weeks being right next to the shepherd. During that time, the sheep learn the shepherd's voice and feel the shepherd's staff as he uses it to guide them and keep them close. But ultimately, the sheep learn to completely trust and rely on the shepherd so when the temptation to run away comes, they remain close to the shepherd.

As a widow, I can easily identify as that sheep. I often feel lost, broken, and in need of an escape plan. Life is overwhelming and distracting, and I can easily be led astray or refuse to be led anywhere, wanting the safety and comfort that is found in the escape of sleep, mind numbing TV, or endless chores.

Psalm 23:1 tells us, "The Lord is my shepherd; I shall not want." But I want so much! I want what I had and not what lays before me. But read on! It goes on to say how the Good Shepherd leads us, restores us, and takes away fear and how He is with us. How His gentle guiding is a comfort, and He is so powerful that He helps us overcome those who would be against us. Verse 6 states, "Surely goodness and mercy shall follow me all the days of my life, and I shall dwell in the house of the Lord forever."

Dear hurting and vulnerable widow, just like the sheep, you have a Good Shepherd who wants to guide and protect you, to teach you to hear His voice, and to help you navigate your steps so you can avoid complications in your future. He has a plan for your future that is filled with goodness. Learn to trust in Him!

Prayer: Lord, help us to trust You even when we are walking in the valley of the shadow of death. Show us Your goodness and mercy today.

Perspective: It's sometimes easy to want to run away from our Good Shepherd, feeling as if He has not been good to us. This only leads to more heartache and potential dangers to our lives. We need to lean into God and trust His will for our lives.

Prompt: Is it hard for you to think of God as your Good Shepherd? Take this time to write down the good things in your life. Are you blessed with children? Do you have the shelter of a home? How about food and clothes? Start with the small things, and open your eyes to the goodness of God in your life. I think you will find that He has been a Good Shepherd to you.

32

Brave

(Sharon)

He will wipe away every tear from their eyes.
There will be no more death
or mourning or crying or pain, for the old
order of things has passed away.
Revelation 21:4 NIV

Today was a day I dreaded. I needed to get a lab test done for my doctor. I had put off going for three months because this was the same lab I had visited every week for two years with my husband for his lab work.

As I walked through the door, I told myself to be brave. Memories were swimming around in my head as I thought of all the times I had sat in this room with Don. When my name was called, I followed the young lab technician back to room four. It had always been my husband who got in the chair and laid his arm out for the poking and prodding. But today it was my turn.

I think I would have been okay had the technician not asked how I was doing. Immediately, tears welled up in my eyes, and I shared with her that I had recently lost my husband. She was very kind with her words of condolence. After the lab draw, I quickly gathered my belongings, praying I could get to my car before I completely lost control of my emotions.

I have discovered grief is hard work and exhausting and unpredictable. You never know when it will surface—when it will suddenly sweep over you with pain and hurt.

I love what Revelation 21:4 tells us—that one day there will be no more pain or sorrow or tears. What a wonderful truth this is, bringing comfort to hurting hearts. God has written the last chapter, and one day there will be eternal joy for those who love God. It's a promise.

Prayer: *Heavenly Father,* help me as I walk through this time of grieving the loss of my husband. Thank You for Your promise that someday my tears will be wiped away, and I will experience eternal joy in heaven.

Perspective: For those of us who have accepted Jesus Christ as our Savior, what lies ahead of us after this life is wonderful! We can confidently look forward to heaven, where there will be no more sorrow and no more tears.

Prompt: Take time and read Revelation 21:4. Write the promises God has given in this verse. Even in your pain and tears, thank God for His promises. Read them over and over. Believe them and claim them as your own.

33

Joy
(Lori)

The thief comes only to steal,
and kill and destroy.
I came that they may have life
and have it abundantly.
John 10:10

"They can't steal my joy!" was a phrase my husband often used. Though his body failed him and his voice grew weak, he was always joyful. After he passed, I so easily let my joy be stolen. In a lot of ways, I *wanted* to be sad and miserable. Eventually, I got sick of being sick of my sad self and went on a mission to find joy in life again.

When you have Jesus in your life, you also receive the Holy Spirit who lives inside you and provides you with certain things: love, joy, peace, patience, gentleness, kindness, and self-control. Because I have the Holy Spirit,

I knew I had joy, but I had just put it on mute. As I purposed to find the joy of life again, I decided to start small. I would choose to be happy when spending time with my kids. Then I ventured out and did the same with friends and family. I got back into reading my Bible and took time to sing praise songs to the Lord. Slowly, the joy I had given away returned to me.

Joy isn't dependent upon the circumstances of life; joy is the abundance of God's goodness, grace, and love in our lives. As I started to count my blessings (there were many) and spend time with God, joy flowed naturally.

The end of John 10:10 is the best part: "I came that they may have life and have it *abundantly*." Jesus wants you to have a full and joyful life—an abundant life. If you find yourself in a place of helplessness, hopelessness, or lack of joy in your life, let me encourage you that it's not too late for you to take it back. Focus on what is left in your life and not on what is lost. If you're reading this, then God has a purpose for you and that, my dear friend, is a blessing!

Joy

Prayer: *Lord,* give us joy back in our lives. Help us to count our blessings and not what binds us to despair.

Perspective: This life wants to steal our joy away from us, and when we are in a weak and vulnerable state, sometimes we just give it away. However, it's not too late to get it back!

Prompt: Have you let your joy be stolen? Take a moment and listen to one of your favorite worship songs. One of my favorites is "Good Grace" by Hillsong United. Ask God to fill you with His joy as you worship Him. Take a moment and write down the things in your life that give you joy.

34
Grace
(Sharon)

And He has said to me,
"My grace is sufficient for you,
for power is perfected in weakness."
Most gladly, therefore, I will rather boast
about my weaknesses, so that
the power of Christ may dwell in me.
2 Corinthians 12:9 NASB

It is Saturday again. The wind is gently blowing out-side, and the forecast predicts another extremely hot summer day. These warmer months used to be filled with anticipation of travel, swimming, barbeques, and family gatherings. We spent many summers when the children were young traveling to camps and conferences where Don was the guest speaker. As we became empty nesters, the summers were filled with even more travel. We would often do mission work in Eastern Europe, adding a few days on the end for an enjoyable vacation.

Now I live with memories and beginning to adjust to life alone. In these early days and months of grief, I often felt I would never feel joy again. The house was quiet, and I missed interaction with Don, chatting about the small everyday events of life. Loneliness is a constant companion. In the Bible, we are told that Paul suffered. It was called a thorn in the flesh—a constant companion to him. We are not told what the thorn was. In his pain and his crying out to God to take it away, God had a message for Paul. It was a message of grace for him then, and it is a message of grace for me now.

What is grace? It is God's provision for my struggle of loneliness. As I cry out to God in my loneliness, God's promise to me is, "My grace is sufficient for you." Our God is "the God of all grace" (1 Peter 5:10) and His throne is a "throne of grace" (Hebrews 4:16). God gives enough grace for each day to feel His comfort, and it is sufficient.

Grace

Prayer: *Heavenly Father*, I come to You so needy, asking You to abundantly supply me today with Your grace for my broken heart.

Perspective: God's grace is like a soothing balm on a painful sore, easing the hurt and allowing us the opportunity to heal.

Prompt: God wants His grace to be sufficient for you. In your grief and loneliness, pull God closer instead of pushing Him away from you. Journal today about what is causing you the most pain, and ask God to overwhelm you with His grace.

35

Faith

(Lori)

Remember those who led you,
who spoke the word of God to you;
considering the result of their conduct,
imitate their faith.
Hebrews 13:7 NASB (1995)

*O*ften, when we experience hard things in life, well-meaning people will say something like, "Just keep the faith." This platitude is always offered as an encouragement. However, it is a lot harder to "keep the faith" when you had faith God was going to do one thing but He did something else instead.

I can't tell you how many times I prayed that God would heal my husband. I still believe that if it were God's plan, He definitely would have healed Greg. But that was not the plan, and it wasn't for lack of faith. On this side of death, it is sometimes hard to keep the faith.

Hebrews is an awesome book in the Bible that describes what faith looks like. In chapter 11, the author offers a list of many great people of faith from the Old Testament. When you really look closer at their lives, you see that they were not perfect. There is a lot of heartache and suffering that these people experienced, and yet God gives them a shout-out in Hebrews. So how did they do it? They chose to believe in God no matter what circumstances came into their lives. My husband used to wisely say, "Believe your beliefs and doubt your doubts," yet so often we believe our doubts and doubt our beliefs!

I love the encouragement we get in Hebrews 13:7. Pick a person of great faith and really look into their lives. I'm sure they experienced some sort of setback and loss in their lives, but they kept their eyes on God and didn't waiver in what they knew to be true about Him. He is good and faithful. We can trust Him!

A great way to experience this in your own life is to keep a journal. This is why we are asking you to journal in this book! Write down those things you are asking God for, and remember to come back and write down how He answered your prayers. You will find that God is more than faithful, and trusting Him with your life isn't as tough as you imagined.

Prayer: Lord, help us to follow the example of those who have gone before us and had great faith in You. Personally show us that You are faithful.

Perspective: Knowing godly mentors is a great way to learn how to navigate our own lives. We should observe how they put their faith in God and try to imitate and practice their behaviors.

Prompt: Who in your own life do you admire for their steadfast Christian walk? What habits and characteristics do they exemplify that you can model in your own life? Write down these traits that you admire. Pray if you should ask them to mentor you in your spiritual life, and if you have no one whom you can think of, pray that God would bring someone along who could help you grow in your faith.

36

Remembrance

(Sharon)

*And we know that in all things
God works for the good of those
who love him, who have been called
according to his purpose.*
Romans 8:28 NIV

As the first anniversary of Don's passing was drawing close, I was feeling anxious. Did I want to be alone, perhaps re-reading the sympathy cards and looking at pictures of our life together? Pondering the day, I knew being alone would not be good. I wanted to be with my family where we would share family stories and memories together. I wanted the day to be one of good memories.

As everyone came for the evening of remembrance, my home was bustling with my children, grandchildren, and great-grandchildren. I ordered pizza from Don's favorite pizza place, and after we ate, we gathered in the family room to watch the video my son had made for Don's memorial service. It was filled with a lifetime of memories, and there were lots of "I remember" stories as we watched and reminisced the years. We laughed and we cried.

When the video ended, my six-year-old great-grandson, Peter, jumped to his feet and said, "I want to pray!" A little child shall lead them is exactly what happened. Peter stood in front of the TV as though it had become the stage. He bowed his little head, folded his hands, and began to pray. It was straight from his heart, thanking God for Papa, how much we loved him, and asking God to please, please not let Papa forget us.

As you can imagine, we were all crying by the end of the prayer. It truly was a night to remember. Don would have loved the evening.

In today's Scripture, Romans 8:28 gives us a huge promise. It doesn't say God makes bad things good, but it does say that in all situations He works for the good of those who love Him. He often surprises me when good things happen out of what I thought was going to be a difficult day. His love for us is amazing, and He knows exactly how to bring us encouragement and hope.

Prayer: *Heavenly Father,* thank You for the surprises You give me when I am dreading a hard day. Help me to trust you that You do work *all* things for our good, even the bad.

Perspective: The one-year anniversary of your spouse's death can be challenging to walk through. My suggestion is that you try and prepare ahead of time to think about how you want to remember and honor them on this day, and then pray that God does something miraculous out of the pain.

Prompt: Write down your thoughts about how you want to spend your spouse's death anniversary. Maybe this isn't your first one, but let's be honest, each one of them are difficult. Pray and ask God to give you wisdom on how to spend your day, and then come back and write what you did and how God comforted you.

37

Purpose
(Lori)

"For I know the plans I have for you,"
declares the Lord, "plans to prosper you
and not to harm you, plans to
give you hope and a future."
Jeremiah 29:11 NIV

Before becoming a widow, I knew who I was. I got my degree in education, then moved on to become a mother, and then worked at our church in the worship/creative department and message planning with Greg. When he got sick, I became a full-time caregiver. Together, we stepped down from leading our church, but I was so busy actively trying to help him stay alive that I didn't feel the absence. Once he was gone, all I had left was being a mom, and beyond that, I had no idea who I was or what I was meant to do.

As I started to evaluate where to go next in life, I struggled to find a purpose. Thankfully, my kids were there to motivate me to try and look for something new, but all I really wanted was what I'd had. I really didn't care to know a new purpose for my life. I would try and think about where I belonged in this world, and all the insecurities about who I was started creeping in. Greg and I had been successful in life, but what if *he* was the one who possessed all of the talent? He had a bigger-than-life personality, and I like to stay in the background. How could God use me to do anything in life without Greg? We were a team—we were better together, and no matter how much I wished for that life again, it wasn't what God had in store for me.

Jeremiah 29:11 (NIV) says, "'For I know the plans I have for you,' declares the Lord, 'plans to prosper you and not to harm you, plans to give you hope and a future.'"

Through some time in counseling, I was able to recognize my insecurities and realize that I can't move forward in life when I'm always looking to the past. Maybe you, too, are having a hard time moving forward. Here's a reminder: Our best days are in front of us! God knows us, and He has gifted us uniquely for our circumstances. If we are still breathing, He has a plan and a purpose for us. Don't give up! Pray that God would lead you to know your purpose.

Prayer: Lord, show us Your plan and purpose for our lives. Help us to plainly see it and to keep walking toward it and to never give up.

Perspective: It's easy to have insecurities when losing a spouse and not know how to move forward. The important part is that you take the steps to realize you have a future and not just a past. God has a plan and purpose for your life, uniquely molded just for you.

Prompt: Where do you find yourself today? Are you struggling with what God has planned for your future? Take some time and pray that God would reveal some forward momentum steps for you to take. Write those steps down, and then put together a game plan for how you can start taking those steps.

38

Plan

(Sharon)

*Being confident of this, that he who began
a good work in you will carry it on to
completion until the day of Jesus Christ.*
Philippians 1:6 NIV

As a young woman in college, I was asked to share
dorm devotions a few months after arriving. I
chose this Philippians verse, and then I took it as my guiding verse for my life.

Now, as an older woman, I ask myself if I'm going to
trust God that His plan is still perfect and good since my
husband has gone to heaven. Truthfully, I struggle with
"who am I?" I loved being known as Don's wife—of hearing our names used together. Don was such a gigantic
part of my identity. There was protection in being one
with him. I feel incomplete because half of me is missing.

The one who walked with me, held me in his loving arms, and whispered daily, "I love you," are now memories.

Philippians 1:6 reminds me that God has not forgotten me as a widow. He knows the early days of being alone are hard. He's not tired of my tears of sadness and crying out for help. He has a plan and will continue working it out throughout all my life. So I try to remember that in this new season the things happening to me are not outside God's knowledge. He knows, He understands, and He offers an abundance of comfort when I lean on Him, call on Him, and trust Him.

Prayer: *Heavenly Father*, I'm trusting Your words that You started a good work in my life many years ago, and I know You will continue my journey until I see You. I'm choosing to lean into Your comfort, identity, and purpose.

Perspective: We can be confident as widows, even if our spouse's death came as a surprise to us, that God has a wonderful plan for our lives.

Prompt: Are you struggling with God's plan for your life, thinking that you don't like His plan very much and wishing He would change it and give you your spouse back? Realize that God's plan doesn't just involve you, but your spouse, your children, those you know, and really, beyond what you know—God's plan involves the whole world. We won't truly be able to understand God's divine plan, but while we are doing the hard work of walking through pain and grief, the wisest decision we can make is to trust Him and allow Him access into our lives to continue His plan for us. Journal your thoughts to Him and let Him know you are willing to trust Him, or write a prayer, asking God to help you be willing to accept His plan for your life.

39

Heaven

(Lori)

For me to live is Christ,
and to die is gain.
Philippians 1:21

*H*ave you ever really thought about what it must be like in heaven? We are not told a lot about heaven in Scripture, but what we are told makes it sound like a wonderful place. There is no sickness, no death, no pain, no suffering. Those things are only for this life. In heaven, you are in the presence of God almighty. That is mind blowing!

My husband's life verse was Philippians 1:21, "For me to live is Christ, and to die is gain." I once asked Greg as he was lying in a hospital bed if he believed God could heal him. He said, "Absolutely." Then I asked him what would happen if God chose not to heal him. Without hesitation, he said, "I win."

When I really think about the verse Greg chose as his life verse, I am perplexed by the idea that heaven is gain. Here on earth, it feels I am only losing things. I lost the love of my life, my kids lost their father, and our church lost their pastor. I am heartbroken that he is gone, but for him, he's only experienced gains. I am heartbroken that we can't grow old together, that he can't watch his kids grow up, and that his life was cut way too short, but somehow, that is gain too. Here on earth, he wanted so badly to stay with us, but now that he is in heaven, what he could've had here on earth is nothing compared to what he has there.

As the one who is left behind, it seems unfair and painful to think that perhaps he has moved on from us down here—that our strong connection is broken. And yet the family is one of God's greatest creations. I don't believe he went to heaven and forgot about us—I think he's getting it warmed up for us. Those bonds we created here are going to be there, but so much more so. Because heaven is gain.

In your heartache, remind yourself of what is to come. Fix your eyes on heaven and all that will be gained and not only on what was lost. The best is yet to come!

Prayer: *Lord*, remind me in my weakest moments of wanting to dwell on what I lost to contemplate the future and what I will gain.

Perspective: We tend to focus on what's lost and not on what's left or what is to come. Let's intentionally focus on what purpose God has us here for, because what's to come is going to be better than we could ever imagine.

Prompt: What do you think your purpose is, and why has God left you here? I know for me, my children are one of my purposes. Write down why you think God has you here, and if you can't think of anything, pray that He would provide you an answer. Ask Him to give you hope and excitement for the future. Remember, your best days are still to come!

40

Goodbye
(Sharon)

*Do not let your hearts be troubled. You believe
in God; believe also in me. My Father's house
has many rooms; if that were not so, would I
have told you that I am going there to prepare
a place for you? And if I go and prepare a
place for you, I will come back and take you to
be with me that you also may be where I am.*
John 14:1–3 NIV

Don only had a few days left to live, and he wanted to be home surrounded by his family. It was
a bittersweet time as family members came to soak up
the last hours with him. To some he was Dad, and to
many, he was Papa. We spent long hours together, singing around his bed, filling the room with music, reading
his favorite Scriptures, and praying. Then heaven slipped
into our bedroom and gently carried him to his eternal

home. His suffering was over. He was and is safely home in the presence of Jesus.

I try to imagine what heaven is like. Jesus told His disciples, who were sad because He was leaving them, to not let their hearts be troubled. He would prepare a place so incredible it was indescribable. He intentionally chose common, physical terms like house, rooms, and places to describe what He was preparing for those who love Him. We are also told in Revelation that there will be no more pain, sorrow, or death. So, my dear widow friend, our goodbye this side of heaven is "see you later."

God has an unimaginable future planned for each one who knows Jesus. So while I continue to live here, I know He's going to take care of my hurting, lonely heart until the day I, too, am home in heaven.

Goodbye

Prayer: *Heavenly Father*, goodbyes are so hard. Please wrap Your loving arms around us and our broken hearts in having said goodbye to our spouses.

—

Perspective: Saying goodbye is never a pleasant experience, but we do have hope of being with Jesus in heaven someday. We need to trust Him with our grief.

—

Prompt: No matter how peaceful the goodbye is, it's still difficult and hard. Maybe your goodbye was anything but peaceful, or maybe you didn't get to say goodbye at all. Jesus's words about not being troubled includes us all. God loves us all so much that He is building a place for us beyond this life. This life is what the Bible calls a "vapor"; it's here and then gone. What we do in this life matters. Are we going to trust God that He has our best in mind? Take some time to write out action steps you can take to put your trust in God for your life. Pray that He would help you take them.

Greg and Lori doing what they loved best—being together (2013)

Sharon and Don loving life together (2017)

Finding Jesus

*I*f you are reading this, searching for how to know Jesus, let me share with you—it's the best decision you can ever make! The Bible tells us in 1 John 5:13 that we can know we have eternal life. Let me explain.

In Romans 6:23, it says that God wants to give us the gift of eternal life, and in Ephesians 2:8–9, the Bible further explains that it truly is a gift—there is nothing we can do to earn or deserve it. The only way to heaven is by accepting this gift from God. We can't be good enough to make it into heaven on our own because we are sinners.

Romans 3:23 states that we all have sinned and have fallen short of God's standard. What is this standard? In Matthew 5:48, the Bible tells us that God is perfect, without flaw or error, and in order to be with Him in heaven, we must meet that standard of perfection. Now we have a problem. We are imperfect. And we need to be perfect in order to be with God—and God solved this problem in the person of Jesus Christ!

When we read through the New Testament of the Bible, we find out who Jesus really is. He is both God and man. Jesus came to this earth and lived a sinless life, experiencing everything that we as humans face, except He did it all without sinning. Then He died on the cross for our sins and rose again, conquering death! By doing both of those things in our place, He made a way for us to get into heaven.

Like all gifts, we have to receive it. And this gift is received by us through faith. This faith must be a saving faith, not just an acknowledgment that we know there is a God, or maybe we shouted a prayer to Him in a time of crisis. This faith must be us relinquishing control of our lives and telling Jesus that we give Him full control. It's us recognizing that we can only get into heaven because of what Jesus did on the cross and transfer our faith from ourselves to Him.

If you are ready to make that decision and ask Jesus to save you and be Lord of your life, pray this prayer after me (it's not the words that are magical in any way. It's the attitude of the heart that counts):

Lord, I am a sinner and I need You. Please come into my life, forgive me of my wrongdoings, and make me a place in heaven where I can spend eternity with You. I transfer my faith from myself, or whatever I was hoping would get me into heaven, and I now put my faith in only You to save me. Thank You for doing what You said You would do and making me acceptable before God. Amen.

Let me be the first to congratulate you on becoming the newest member of heaven! So what should you do now? Tell someone! You can email Lori at lori.beautifullybroken@gmail.com. You might have some questions. A good place to go for those is www.gotquestions.org. They have answers for some of the toughest spiritual questions.

Order Information

To order additional copies of this book, please visit
www.redemption-press.com.
Also available on Amazon.com and BarnesandNoble.com
or by calling toll-free 1-844-2REDEEM.